READy to Sow
Fall Poems for a Spring Audience

PhOEbeTRY

BookLeaf Publishing

India | USA | UK

Presentation by *BookLeaf Publishing*

Web: www.bookleafpub.com

E-mail: info@bookleafpub.com

ISBN: 9789357446853

First edition 2022

ACKNOWLEDGEMENT

To my Mom and Dad: Thank you for everything, then, now, and always.
To my boyfriend: Thank you for supporting my dreams, for all the times you took over when it was my turn to make dinner so I could keep writing, and for making all of this possible.

PREFACE

Yay! It's here: my (first) poetry book, and you're holding it now. I couldn't be more proud of the end result! Sharing my work with you, is absolutely terrifying. Still I jumped at the opportunity to get published. And I'm so deeply grateful I did.

Step into the Light

It's time, it's time
though terrified
no more excuse
to run and hide

The voice inside me
hesitates
tries to stop me:
"Why not wait?!

It's not perfect
first fix this
look at every-
thing you miss!"

My feet are cold
my heart beats fast
feels like it's jumping
through my chest

I take back the reins
fears pushed aside
take to the stage
and step into the light

Parents' Paean

Sailing, we're sailing
each their own boat
the sturdy design
keeps us afloat

As kids we start building
the lucky get two
foremen to guide and
to show us 'how to'

Providing material
high quality wood
soft yet robust
to bend where it should

The boat takes its shape
through sanding and planing
stroke by stroke: lessons
in our life's training

To keep it together
there's glue and there's nails
forgiveness, compassion
for mistakes, fumbles, fails

A layered veneer
has it all sealed
from seas, stormy weather
it offers a shield

We choose our own image
by what color we paint
final layer of varnish
for shine that won't faint

Advanced navigation
an ongoing course
morals and values
knowing safe ports

To reach destinations
a helm gives control
to steer and adjust
towards our goals

Then it's seaworthy
all watertight
time to set sail
for horizons so bright

When my boat was ready
my foremen cheered me on
they wished me 'fair winds!'
knew I'd make it on my own

Though my boat is fully stocked
and carefully packed
I reg'larly sail back
and we always stay connect'd

For while building my boat
our relationship took form
stronger than most violent storm
you're the dock I go back to
grateful for the two of you

You

I love how you gentle
I love how you tough

I love how you on
I love how you off

I love how you brainy
I love how you heart

I love how you silly
I love how you smart

I love how you jazzy
I love how you rock

I love how you silent
I love how you talk

I love how you funny
I love how you stern

I love how you teach
I love how you learn

I love how you ser'ous
I love how crazy

I love how you active
I love how you lazy

I love how you humble
I love how you proud

I love how you quiet
I love how you loud

I love how you stare
I love how you glance

I love how you stand
I love how you dance

I love how you wake
I love how you sleep

I love how you surface
I love how you deep

I love how you ballad
I love how you swing

I love how you hum
I love how you sing

I love how you hear
I love how you see

I love how you you
I love how you me

Be Gentle

Here is my story
pages, lines, words
I'll tell you 'bout happy
I'll leave out the hurt

I'm an open book
yet private and closed
when it comes to the things
that matter the most

My joy I love sharing
my dance and my noise
my surface, my outside
not my deepest voice

Close to my chest
I keep doubts and fears
matters of the heart
I swallow my tears

I'm slow but I'm learning
to open up some more
to sometimes shed a light
on my very core

So, when you get to see
I beg of you please be
considerate and
gentle with me

Take it In

Look at the things you got today
the things you once dreamt of
your business or your first own home
your kids, the one you love

It's tempting to keep wanting
striving for more stuff
more status, bigger, better
and still it ain't enough

'Course we keep on running
working hard to reach our goal
but we just cannot ignore
a marathon can take its toll

Let's not forget to take a beat
to fully 'ppreciate
every milestone we've accomplished
so far, to this date

Not for patting on the back
though being proud's okay
taking in where you are now
before continuing on your way

On and upwards
here we go
more to learn
more to grow

Heart wide open
open mind
looking forward
and sometimes
at the road behind

Old Friends

This is a tribute
to some friends of mine
close to my heart
since my early time

Patsy, Connie, Doris
Peggy and Brenda Lee
faithful companions
part of the family

Perry, Elvis, Frankie
and two guys named Neil
always in my corner
no matter how I feel

Lots of brothers and sisters
Dean, Buddy and Jim
always standing by me
through the thick and thin

Never once a no-show
every holiday
domestic and abroad
until the end of days

Standing invitation
every occasion
or even none at all
they are my first call

Looking In

Inside is family
laughter and friends
getting together
hugs, shaking hands

Inside is cozy
there's love, it feels warm
they're loud and lighthearted
the fireplace's on

Outside is lonely
just me and my voice
my thoughts are all screaming
to drown out the noise

Outside is freezing
quiet and dark
my breath's drawing circles
they're leaving my mark

Outside is silence
no twitter, no song
just to remind me
I'm out here alone

I try to reach out
nose 'gainst the pane
nobody sees me
it's all in vain

Looking from
the outside in
they move to the table
glasses, chin-chin

Pots, plates, platters
for everyone plenty
except for me
my stomach feels empty

I finally manage
to somehow get in
the cabin's dark
the people gone
perhaps it's been
my imagination
…all along

The last Time

When's the last time
no one knows
maybe yesterday

When's the last time
no one knows
could've passed me 'long the way

Did I miss it
wasn't present
I forgot to wave
if I would've been aware
what would I have changed?

Better - Worse

I bet it gets better
but first it gets worse
have to go forward
to read the next verse

Dive right in
brave, headfirst
just go all in
fully immerse

A whole new chapter
will soon emerge
can't skip a page
or go in reverse

We all get one go
no time to rehearse
I bet it gets better
but first it gets worse

Beginnings Blues

It takes courage to begin
even more than follow-through
starting is so daunting
'cause it's 'perfect' I pursue

Not willing to settle
I dread, I postpone
if I keep procrastinating
at least I know I won't

Till it's time to choose:
do nothing, dare to fail
if I put it that way
the latter tips the scale

I'd rather imagine flying
than focus on a fall
that's only in potential
who says I'll fail at all?

So, carefully I go
full fear ahead
stop dragging my feet
and take the first few steps

Once I've actually started
I just have to keep going
keep up the momentum
no more time for slowing

My single greatest challenge
is learning now to trust:
ingredients they all are here
my best is good enough

Time to decide
start doing it for me
nothing left to prove
what if that's the key?

Uneventful

Looking for the special
the famous pot of gold
always chasing 'epic'
the unimaginable

Life-changing adventure
mountain tops, the sky
but what if this idea
is basically a lie

If I'm honest actually
I don't mind mundane
if the choice is up to me
I'd take tea over champagne

Could magic lie in uneventful
simple, daily things
together slouching on our couch
the first kiss in the morning

Don't want to lose one minute
staring at what no one's seen
nothing more than mere mirage
and miss what's right in front of me

Daily Presents

Sun hangs low above the trees
the day comes to an end
she paints her colors in the sky
they just perfectly blend

Pinks, purples, reds and gold
her presents every day
goodbye she waves
her final rays
they gently grace
my face

The Song in the Night

Last night I dreamt up a song
heard verses and chorus
melody and rhyme
in harmony divine
I forgot about time

Every note, every chord
the rhythm and tune
I could just hear the band
each instrument
perfectly blend'd

Such a shame I was sleeping
else I would've held on
it was mine thr'out the night
where it sounded just right
till break of daylight

When I woke up this morning
it still echoed inside
but it slowly distorted
and it's very unfortun'te
I forgot to record it

I begged to come back
tried to retrieve it
kept jogging my mem'ry
so the world, through me,
could know its beauty

Imagine what it'd be like
to hear The Perfect Song
the best ever made
oh, if only its fate
wasn't to just evaporate

Now I've given up searching
for the song in the night
racked my brain
but alas all in vain
so 'the song in the night'
that it remains

Meander

We all have a task on earth
a purpose to fulfill
where we get to thrive,
to use and hone our skills

Some of us know early on
what they have to give
how to make their contribution
to the world in which we live

Others have to really search
to find their destiny
to get to that perfect place
where they're meant to be

No, it's not the quickest route
there's boulders 'long the way
winding, curving, challenging
anything but straight

But like a river unafraid
starting from her source
to get to her destination
dares to change her course

I feel now I can trust
though detours caused delay
that there's no need to rush
I honestly can say
I'm now well on my way

Companions

In life we get companions
we meet along the way
some walk with us a couple miles
others get to stay

They find us at the perfect time
when we have something to learn
and should they need to learn from us
we teach them in return

Our encounters have a reason
we help each other grow
even if we don't know then
that is how it goes

for people that we work with
and our closest friends
even each romance
until the very end

It's why sometimes we lose touch
relationships do fade
people simply drift apart
when their role is played

So next time when we shed a tear
lose sight of who we once held dear
we know they went a new direction
on to new companions
on to a new lesson

Like the Others

Sailor, barber
poor or rich
famous singer
don't mind which

Whether you work
or be a bum
doesn't matter
what you've become

Once we're out here
last breath took
ink dried up
and closed the book

Like de Gaulle
said 'bout his daughter:
"now she's fin'lly
like the others"*

Can't take nothing
to the grave
it's not what you had
but what you gave

Gather mem'ries
not possessions
be the best you
you can be
whatever your profession

* When his daughter who had Down Syndrome
died in 1948, at the funeral Charles de Gaulle
said: "Now she is like the others."

Growth

Young and green
above the ground
little leaves
here I found

Stop and stare
on my knees
closer look
what can it be

How will it grow
what kind of roots
will it bear flowers
or possibly fruit

It takes patience
see and wait
give it time
just appreciate

every phase
stage by stage
to get to full-grown
may cost more days
growing comes
in many ways

Black-and-White

I used to live in color
bright and vibrantly
now everything has faded
just black-and-whites I see

We used to watch together
but then I lost my wife
my son no longer comes around
just walked out of my life

His final letter
I have it here
says: "goodbye, dad!"
painf'lly clear

Still in my heart
but out of sight
out of my life
in black-and-white

The ones I loved
are on my mind
I think of 'em
behind the blinds

So every day
I, all alone,
watch their movies
in my home

Engagement party
candle blowing
the Christmas when
she first start'd showing

His first few steps
I can watch all night
over and over
in black-and-white

On my walls and dressers
the desk where I write
all fam'ly portraits
in black-and-white

I surround myself
with what reminds
me of the loved ones
left behind

Silent movies
black-and-white
silent witness'
of a once
colorful life

Nothing

Floating between
here and there
feels like I'm
not anywhere

No solid ground
I stretch my feet
just more nothing
there to meet

I keep on reaching
there's not even clouds
I try to scream
nothing comes out

Stuck out here
nowhere to go
neither up nor down
just keep afloat!

Be the Light

If someone's struggling daily
if all they see is night
then let me be a beacon
let me be the light

A simple smile or gesture
a genuine 'how are you?'
with your act of kindness
the light can shine through you

Remember we may never
know how someone feels
behind a mask of happy
can be sad, for real

Let's show 'em that we're out here
ready when they are
our hand there for the taking
never very far

We can make a difference
by op'ning up our eyes
to those who just might need us
by being by their side
by list'ning to their story
we can be the light

Inspiration

So here is my confession:
I regu'rly get caught
stuck within a web of words
all tangled up in knots

But thankfully I sometimes get
help from mysterious source
they call it 'inspiration'
it's send to reinforce

Like many wordsmiths 'round the world
in books, poems, and songs
I'll try to put it into words
this exceptional phenomenon

To me it's like a blessing
that magically appears
it suddenly reveals itself
a whisper in my ear

It tells me to just follow
to turn off my own mind
to listen with my heart
and leave all else behind

Somehow it takes me over
it hurries me along
I barely can keep up
but never steers me wrong

Elusive, fascinating
we may never comprehend
do know where we'd be without it:
stages, museums, lib'ries
would all be empty and…
these pages would be blank